WHAT IS A
Family?

SOME OTHER BOOKS BY VARDELL & WONG

What Is a FRIEND?

Things We Do

Things We Eat

Things We Feel

GREAT MORNING:
Poems for School Leaders to Read Aloud

HERE WE GO:
A Poetry Friday Power Book

HOP TO IT:
Poems to Get You Moving

The Poetry Friday Anthology
for Celebrations

The Poetry of Science

YOU JUST WAIT:
A Poetry Friday Power Book

WHAT IS A
Family?

by
Sylvia Vardell
+
Janet Wong

Pomelo
Books

100% of the profits from this book will be donated to the IBBY Children in Crisis Fund.

The IBBY Children in Crisis Fund provides support for children whose lives have been disrupted through war, civil disorder, or natural disaster. The program gives immediate support and help — and also aims for long-term community impact, aligning with IBBY's goal of giving every child the right to become a reader.

ibby.org/awards-activities/ibby-children-in-crisis-fund
usbby.org/donate.html

IBBY
by Janet Wong

IBBY is a family with books in our bones.
We think of stories and poems
when we eat, when we walk,
when we drift to sleep, when we dream.

We don't see each other
as often as we would like.
But even when we are not in the same place,
we worry together.
We support each other.

Like all families, we have our differences, but
when the day is done, we always agree:
children need books,
the best we can find, so they can thrive
sheltered by walls of words,
warmed by windows of hope.

This book is dedicated to supporters of IBBY all over the world.

Special thanks to Renée M. LaTulippe for her ongoing help in editing Pomelo Books publications.

Pomelo Books
9440 Viewside Drive
Dallas, TX 75231
PomeloBooks.com
info@pomelobooks.com

Text/compilation copyright © 2023 by Pomelo Books. All rights reserved.
Individual poems copyright © 2023 by the individual poets. All rights reserved.
Photos sourced from Canva.com.
Library of Congress Cataloging-in-Publication Data is available.
ISBN 978-1-937057-19-0

Please visit us at PomeloBooks.com

POEMS BY

Alma Flor Ada

Gail Aldous

Alexia M. Andoni

Chris Baron

Willeena Booker

Sandy Brehl

Judy Bryan

Elenore Byrne

F. Isabel Campoy

Kate Coombs

Cynthia Cotten

Mary E. Cronin

Leslie Degnan

Janet Clare Fagal

Theresa Gaughan

Rajani LaRocca

Renée M. LaTulippe

Rebecca Gardyn Levington

Molly Lorenz

Rochelle Melander

Jack Prelutsky

Joan Riordan

Donna JT Smith

Anastasia Suen

Pamela Taylor

Joyce Uglow

Fernanda Valentino

April Halprin Wayland

Vicki Wilke

Matthew Winter

Janet Wong

Helen Kemp Zax

TABLE OF CONTENTS

TABLE OF CONTENTS

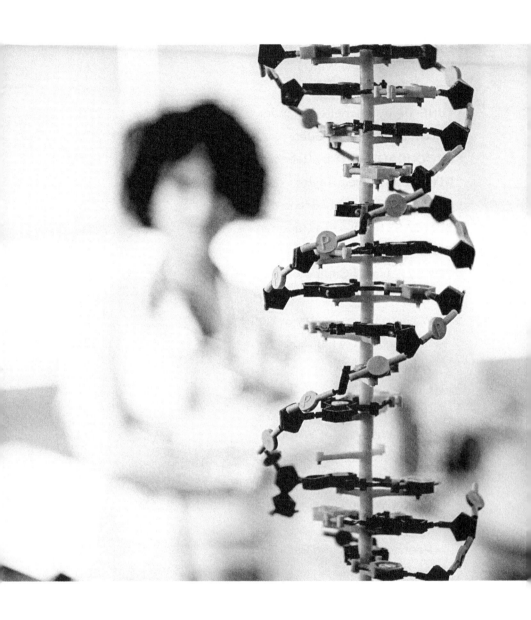

FAMILY

by Rajani LaRocca

Family can share DNA,
chromosomes, and genes.
But shared genetics is only part
of what *family* can mean.

Family means time together,
laughter over meals,
a hug, a kiss, a squeezing hand –
that's how family feels.

Some families all look alike.
Some share no DNA.
But all share love through good and bad.
That's the family way.

REUNION

by Willeena Booker

We squeeze in tight
loving hearts fill the frame

Gathered from far and near
to celebrate our family name

Gramps is sitting
right next to me

Our beautiful family
celebrating unity

Our reunion brings
family cheer

Laughter and loved ones
my favorite time of year

WEDDING

by Renée M. LaTulippe

On this starry summer night
my aunt married
my new uncle

we enfold them
in a hug formed
of family

the night shines bright
with starry eyes

we dance

I twirl my sparkler high
making my own stars

lighting up
love

COUSINS

by Mary E. Cronin

We've got cousins
by the dozen
buzzing about
at Saturday playtime
or Sunday cookout.
We lean on each other,
we tickle and poke.
We tell funny stories.
We argue and joke.
We may not look the same
as we're laughing
and playing.
Love makes a family –
that's all that I'm saying.

WE

by Alma Flor Ada

Tía María brought some seedlings.
Tío Juan helped to plant them.
My sister and I made sure
they were always watered.

Now they are on a large basket
over Grandma's kitchen table.
A large pumpkin, some string beans,
red tomatoes and green peppers,
sweet corn and spicy radishes,
carrots, lettuce, zucchini.

I shout, "Like a family!"
and everyone is surprised.
"Yes," I say, "look at them:
large and small,
round and skinny,
sweet and spicy,
and all those colors . . .
each adding a unique flavor.
Just like our family!"

SHARING

by Janet Wong

When we go for dim sum
we choose such different things.
My grandmother: sweet sesame balls.
My mother: tough tripe.
My cousin: soft custard buns.
Me: salty shrimp dumplings.
The food sits in the middle of the table.
Nobody has to take anything
they don't want,
except Grandpa always tries
to make us kids
eat some chicken feet.

"Family style" is all about the sharing:
what will we share today?

CLASSROOM

by April Halprin Wayland

Mom had eleven brothers and sisters.
But me? It's just me.

I ache
for eleven brothers and sisters.
For our house to be just as
messy-happy-crowded-loud.

After a movie,
I sit in a circle with my stuffed animals
and tell them the whole movie,
from start to finish,
just like Mom's oldest sister told her family
because they could only afford one ticket.

Today in class we're showing
how many kids live in our house.
Today I don't care
that I'm only raising one finger.

Because here, in Ms. Escarra's class,
I've found
my messy-happy-crowded-loud
family.

BAND

by Janet Clare Fagal

Some bands play at ball games,
others work hard to compete.
Some perform at concerts,
some parade down the street.
We rehearse and we practice
the songs that we'll play.
Our tubas and drumline
add pep right away!
Our trumpets and trombones
blare the melody line.
Our flutes, horns and piccolos
make all of us shine.
Each musical note in the score
needs another –
our band is a family
of sisters and brothers!

TOGETHER

by Joyce Uglow

We gather.
We huddle.
We play.
"One team," Coach says.
"Let's go!" we cheer.

We look.
We see.
We give.
"Well done!" Coach says.
"Nice pass!" we cheer.

We plan.
We act.
We do.
"Be there," Coach says.
"Together!"

PUPPIES!

by April Halprin Wayland

It could have gone one of two ways:
NO. No way! Pick one and let's go home.
or
Sure, Kiddo – why the heck not?
Tell 'em we'll take the whole kit-n-kaboodle.

I could have had to choose one, just one,
and maybe I would have chosen the licky one
with that big old black eye.
I'd name her Pirate. Biggy Paws.
Or maybe T-Bone.

But it's been a long, long, loooong winter.
It's been bad.
So we drove away with Biggy Paws
and all the rest
and Mama couldn't stop laughing
when we brought them in the door.

CATCH-UP
by Rochelle Melander

I wriggle out of my egg,
wraggle up through the sand,
just to swim home with you.

I scrabble over the shells,
scramble across the dunes.

We'll dive into the sea
catch a wave, swim to safety –
brothers and sisters and me.

ORCAS

by Kate Coombs

With rolling tails
and gleaming sides,
we arc together,
splash and dive.

My brothers play,
my sisters leap,
we hunt for fish,
we arrow deep.

We whistle, click,
and big or small,
we all come
when Mama calls!

Note: Orcas are matrilineal, which means
their families are led by mothers and
grandmothers. Orca calls may seem
similar to humans', but each family group
actually has its own special set of sounds
for communicating. Scientists call these
"dialects."

HIVE

by Donna JT Smith

We're buzzing, sometimes humming,
such excitement in our lives.
Every one of us is busy
as the bees that build their hives.
We fly off to our work or school,
then sports and other meetings,
and all day long we flit around
to things that need completing,
until at last we zzz-ooo-mmm back home,
our place to congregate.
Together with our family
we share and contemplate
the day's events and BUZZYness
until we've all unwound,
then take our rest in quietness
till morning comes around.

Though busy, busy as a bee,
we still return to family!

CHORES

by Molly Lorenz

My family works together
by doing each one's chores.
We have responsibilities
both outdoors and indoors.

My mother buys the groceries and
my father cooks the meals.
My brother dries the dishes and
I wash them.

That's our deal.

GRANNY

by Cynthia Cotten

Dad says our car is like a member of our family.
He even calls her "Granny,"
because she's getting old.

Granny takes us where we want to go,
where we need to go.
She keeps us safe.

We take care of Granny. We wash and wax her,
make sure she doesn't go hungry,
make sure she has regular checkups.

Granny's not as pretty as some other cars.
Her paint has a few scars and scratches.
She doesn't go as fast.

But she's ours. So I help take care of her
because I hope
she'll be with us for a long, long time.

STORYTIME

by Elenore Byrne

My granny lives far
across oceans and seas
where tui birds sing
in the totara trees.

I miss her pink slippers
and chipped coffee mugs,
her half-finished crosswords
and long snuggly hugs.

On Saturday nights
about quarter to nine,
where over the seas,
the morning sun shines,

she reads me a story
and tucks me in tight,
no oceans between us
on Saturday night.

LAUGHTER
by Leslie Degnan

Around the campfire,
Grandpa becomes a philosopher.

"For a good life you need
good food,
good friends,
family,
and laughter."

"But Grandpa, what about all of this?"
I ask, sweeping both hands above me,
all around me.

Grandpa is quiet.

Together we look up
at the vastness of the Milky Way.
We breathe in the quiet,
the scent of pine on the night air.

Grandpa sighs and says,
"You also need . . .
the stars above your head,
the earth beneath your feet,
and a grandson to remind you."

We laugh together.

GRANDMA

by Jack Prelutsky

I'm visiting my grandma,
She's always a delight.
She tells me scary stories
That keep me up all night.
Her cooking is delectable,
She makes treat after treat,
Then feeds me food my parents say
I'm not supposed to eat.

Sometimes she takes me to the park,
And sometimes to the zoo.
She seems to know the animals,
They seem to know her too.
She helped me learn to ride a bike,
To swim and fly a kite.
I simply love to visit her,
She's always a delight.

HANDSHAKE

by Leslie Degnan

We need a secret handshake,
for every time we meet.
One just for the four of us,
that no one else can know.

It starts out with a fist bump,
plus a proper shake.
A high five and a low five,
and then a double shake.

Ready? Want to try it?

A fist bump and a shake.
High five and a low five.
Grandpa, don't play tricks –
You pulled your hand away!

I'm trying not to laugh,
but this is too much fun.
Could we add a clap?
A hip bump would be good.

Fist bump, handshake,
high five, low five,
double shake, hip bump,
clap and done!

BALANCE
by Joan Riordan

playFul
nudging
give And
take
Mindful
maneuvers
contInuous
adjustment
deLicate
balance
hIghs
and lows
hElping
hands
suStaining
stability

Note: The game name *Jenga* is derived from
kujenga, a Swahili word which means "to build."

ROOTS
by Chris Baron

When Grandpa was little,
he planted a tree.
Every year he brings us to see it,
the branches opening wide
beneath the endless sky.
"Our family is like this tree," he says,
"each of us a branch,
each a little different,
each its own shape
going in its own direction,
bearing its own fruit."

But all the branches
are still part of one trunk
attached to deep roots
that are stronger than the branches,
more solid than the trunk
winding through the wide world
     far away
         yet always
             always connected.

GROVE

by Alexia M. Andoni

My family, like the trees you see,
is a special treasure trove.
Although each tree is quite unique,
combined, they form a grove.

Some limbs have lumps, some bark is smooth,
some leaves turn red or gold,
but underground their roots entwine,
supporting new and old.

And even in the toughest times –
on days when all seems wrong –
just like the grove can weather storms,
together, we are strong.

TROOP

by Judy Bryan

I have their back,
and they have mine.
Strong in solidarity.

We help.
We share.
We grow.
We care.
My trusty scouting family.

EXPECTING
by Vicki Wilke

Hello baby, hello?
Mama says you know my voice.
I have so much to tell you.

I am singing my favorite songs
so you will learn them.
Then we can sing together.

You are growing and growing
in Mama's belly.
I can't wait to hug.

Hello baby, hello.
I am smiling.
Are you smiling, too?

SMOOCHEROOS
by Fernanda Valentino

Raspberry kisses make me giggle.
Smoochy kisses make me wriggle.
Butterfly kisses tickle my nose.
Slobbery-dog kisses wet my toes!
Every kiss says, "I love you!"
My kiss back says, "Love you too!"

WISH

by Helen Kemp Zax

My mother, brother, cousins crow
    their faces lit in candle glow,
    they cheer, *Woo-hoo!* –
       I wish, then blow.

I wish my life could always stay
    exactly as it is today,
    my wish come true –
       one breath away.

CAROUSEL

by Donna JT Smith

Day by day, year by year,
minutes and hours go by;
slowly, slowly at the start,
but later speed up and fly!

That's what my Auntie Ellie says,
and she should know it's true;
there are so many things she knows,
and she will tell you, too!

Auntie Ellie has grown very wise,
she's an expert at most things.
She's almost twelve, I'm only ten.
What knowledge two years bring!

I wish I were someone's old aunt.
I'd tell them stuff I learned:
like how years are a carousel
that turns and turns and turns.

SEARCHING

by Janet Wong

Yesterday
my biggest problem
was figuring out what to eat
for my four o'clock snack
and which game to play –

but today
my whole world has been turned
upside-down.
I cannot believe it.
I keep thinking *no, no, no.*
I am searching for answers.

In my closet
there is a present
I never got to give.

GOODBYE

by Janet Wong

I hadn't seen my uncle for a long time
until yesterday at the hospital –
we've been too busy.
My other uncles and aunts
and lots of cousins I don't even know
were there.
Three of them asked me,
"Who are you?"

Our family only gets together
when something bad happens.
We see them at the hospital.
At the funeral.
Then we go home.
So they don't know me.
They've only seen my sad face.
They've never really heard me talk.
They've only heard me whisper goodbye
in quiet halls.

I think we'd feel more like a family,
if only we could try to be friends.

HOPE

by Matthew Winter

In lieu of flowers, please send:
love
peace
comfort
joy
or
harmony

And –
if you can spare –
maybe a little bit of
hope

for our family

STUFFIES

by Joan Riordan

When I was young,
you'd fill my bed.
Lambs. Llamas. Bunnies. Bears.
You'd barely know
a kid was there.
But I knew you were there –
comforting, protecting, consoling.

Now, piled in a corner of my room,
you still bring peace.

TUNE-UP

by Rochelle Melander

I stall in shop class,
sputter in gym,
idle rough by nightfall.
If I had a check engine light,
it'd be on.

Mom says
everything needs a tune-up
now and then,
engines,
friends,
family,
me.

TUTOR

by Anastasia Suen

Taking time to help me
Understand
To be here
Once again
Right by my side

ENCOURAGEMENT

by Rebecca Gardyn Levington

You cheer for me, inspire me
to be the best that I can be,
and when I'm low or want to cry
your words remind me: I can fly.
You lift me up. You have no doubt.
"You've got this! Yes, you can!" you shout.

Because of you, and all you do,
I'm starting to believe it too.

RIVALS

by Pamela Taylor

Crashing, bashing, whacking, smacking,
two big brothers start attacking.

Horns to horns and toes to toes,
instinct leads them by the nose.

They jab and kick as they prepare
to face their rivals, take a dare.

Through it all, they're undeterred.
Their aim is to protect the herd.

FORECAST

by Sandy Brehl

Distant rumbles signal storms.
Lightning flashes,
strikes my heart,
twists Sister's gut.

We shelter side by side.
Me, watchful.
Her, sullen,
surprised by sunshine's sudden
disappearance.

Storms come and go.
We've been through worse.
I let her know
I'll stay at her side.

SUITCASE

by Theresa Gaughan

I hold her world inside -
the purple t-shirt with the unicorn picture,
the well-worn jeans with the hole in the knee,
the soft pajamas she loves to sleep in,
silly socks, school shoes, and sneakers,
a stuffie for bedtime,
her favorite books and toys.

I carry them safely
between two houses,
so she always feels she's home.

GLAD
by Gail Aldous

A small hand slips into my hand.
A smaller hand slips into my other hand.
My new sister and my new brother smile at me.
We are hiking to their big rock.

The woods smell like holiday candles.
They point to deer that leap,
waving their fluffy white tails.
Wow, I've only seen deer in books!

Where is our big rock, he asks.
She says it's up ahead.
Arriving at the big rock I say, *It's a boulder!*

My sister and brother nap
nestling each other like kittens.
If this is what a family is –
small hands in mine,
laughter, love,
I am
glad.

JOY

by F. Isabel Campoy

Family is the joy
of all for one
and one for all

. . . is a yummy meal
of secret ingredients
hidden in grandma's hands

. . . is a song
learned on summer trips
in mom's old van

. . . is a smile
rushing towards you
if you are sitting lonely and alone

. . . is a place to return to,
where people I love live,
and where they love me back.

RESOURCES
FOR
READERS
AND
WRITERS

WAYS TO SHARE POETRY AT HOME

Here are a dozen simple ways for families to include poetry in the daily routine at home, from sharing a poem at breakfast to recording a favorite poem for a friend or family member far away.

1. Start the day with a poem at breakfast.

2. Add a poem to a lunch bag.

3. Keep a book of poetry in the car and take turns reading out loud.

4. Look for poems on your cell phone or tablet when waiting.

5. Celebrate each birthday with a special poem.

6. Write a poem on the sidewalk with chalk.

7. Listen online to poems performed by the poets.

8. Write a poem together as a gift for a special occasion.

9. Record a poem to share with a friend or family member far away.

10. Listen to songs on the radio and talk about how they are alike or different from poetry.

11. Just for fun, sing a silly poem together.

12. End the day with a poem at dinner or at bedtime.

SHARING POETRY OUT LOUD

It can be fun to read these poems aloud as a group using various informal theater or simple performance techniques.

Simple props can add fun to sharing a poem with a group or larger audience. You can use a common object mentioned in the poem as your "poetry prop" and hold it up while reading aloud. For example, for the poems "Classroom" (p. 21) or "Stuffies" (p. 69), bring a stuffed animal as your poetry prop, or for "Suitcase" (p. 81), your prop can be a suitcase.

Consider using audio sound effects or music as a backdrop for a poem reading, where appropriate. For the poems "Wedding" (p. 13) or "Band" (p. 23), play an appropriate musical clip (of wedding music or a marching band) before or during the reading of the poems. One source of sounds and sound effects is SoundCloud.com.

A poem that employs italicized text can be the perfect opportunity for an interactive read-aloud, with a leader or narrator reading most of the poem and others reading the italicized text for added emphasis.

Whenever dialogue occurs in a poem, a leader can read most of the poem aloud, with volunteers taking on the parts of dialogue. Take a moment to clarify whose line is whose, highlighting the text if that's helpful. Think about making a podcast recording of the reading, too.

Invite guest readers to join you for the oral reading of a poem to add vocal variety. For example, several of the poems in this book feature a grandmother or grandfather, and that provides a perfect opportunity to invite our elders to read a poem out loud with us.

WEB RESOURCES

Here are some websites that offer engaging activities and helpful resources for families. Dive in and have fun!

Colorín Colorado
Colorincolorado.org
*Bilingual activities and advice for educators and families of English language learners (ELLs).

Every Child a Reader
everychildareader.net
*Info about book creators, literacy tools and resources, Kids' Book Choice Awards.

Kidlit TV
kidlit.tv
*Videos highlight brand new books and the authors and illustrators who created them.

No Water River
by Renée M. LaTulippe
NoWaterRiver.com
*Watch videos of poets reading and talking about their poetry.

Poetry for Kids
by Kenn Nesbitt
Poetry4Kids.com
*A "poetry playground" with funny poems.

Poetry Foundation
PoetryFoundation.org
*Sponsor of the Young People's Poet Laureate program, with a searchable database that includes some poems for young people.

The Poetry Minute
PoetryMinute.org
*You'll find a poem for every day, Monday through Friday, from September through June.

EKPHRASTIC POETRY BOOKS

The books on this list feature poetry written in response to art, called "ekphrastic" poetry.

Brenner, Barbara. Ed. 2000. *Voices: Poetry and Art from Around the World.*
*Poems representing six continents focus on culture, history, or land through art.

Greenberg, Jan. 2001. *Heart to Heart: New Poems Inspired by Twentieth-Century American Art.*
*Paintings, sculpture, and photographs by 20th-century American artists inspire these poems.

Greenberg, Jan. 2008. *Side by Side: New Poems Inspired by Art from Around the World.*
*Poems in their original language and in English accompany global art from ancient Egypt to modern Sweden.

Hopkins, Lee Bennett. Ed. 2018. *World Make Way: New Poems Inspired by Art from the Metropolitan Museum of Art.*
*Poems by eighteen poets inspired by some of the most popular art in the collection of The Metropolitan Museum.

Lewis, J. Patrick and Yolen, Jane. 2011. *Self-Portrait with Seven Fingers: A Life of Marc Chagall in Verse.*
*Fourteen of Chagall's famous paintings are the inspiration for poems by these two poets.

Rochelle, Belinda. Ed. 2001. *Words with Wings: A Treasury of African-American Poetry and Art.*
*Twenty African American poets explore twenty works of art by African American artists on themes of slavery, racism, and pride.

Vardell, Sylvia and Wong, Janet. 2022. *Things We Eat.*
*Poets use photo prompts to explore a wide variety of foods from avocados to kimchi to quiche to zucchini.

Vardell, Sylvia and Wong, Janet. 2022. *What Is a Friend?*
*Poets use photo prompts to explore the many dimensions of friendship.

POETRY BOOKS ABOUT FAMILY

The family unit is such an important part of the lives of children as they're developing. Poetry can capture familiar experiences and emotions and celebrate the good times as well as reflect the special challenges of family relationships. Here is a selection of poetry books about families.

Alarcón, Francisco X. 2005. *Poems to Dream Together/Poemas para soñar juntos.*
*Alarcón focuses on family and community through bilingual poems about dreams and goals.

Anholt, Catherine and Laurence Anholt. 1998. *Big Book of Families.*
*A wide variety of family members and family experiences are celebrated in lively poems.

Fletcher, Ralph J. 1999. *Relatively Speaking: Poems about Family.*
*Poetry captures the trials and tribulations of ordinary family life.

George, Kristine O'Connell. 2011. *Emma Dilemma: Big Sister Poems.*
*Fun poems reflect the highs and lows of relationships between sisters.

Grandits, John. 2007. *Blue Lipstick: Concrete Poems.*
*Shape poems explore the up-and-down relationship between a teenage girl and her younger brother.

Greenfield, Eloise. 2022. *Brothers & Sisters: Family Poems.*
*Poems that celebrate the special relationship between siblings.

Grimes, Nikki. 1999. *Hopscotch Love: A Family Treasury of Love Poems.*
*Poems celebrate family love and traditions in the African American community.

Gunning, Monica. 2013. *A Shelter in Our Car.*
*A mother and daughter experiencing homelessness show love and determination.

Harrison, David. 2009. *Vacation: We're Going to the Ocean!*
*All about a big family vacation road trip.

Harrison, David L. 2018. *A Place to Start a Family: Poems About Creatures That Build.*
*Science-based poetry features animal families and their homes.

Hoberman, Mary Ann. 2009. *All Kinds of Families.*
*Playful, rollicking rhymes explore all kinds of families and how we grow together.

Hollyer, Belinda. Ed. 2003. *The Kingfisher Book of Family Poems.*
*More than 100 poems explore the diversity of modern family life.

Hopkins, Lee Bennett. 1995. *Been to Yesterdays: Poems of a Life.*
*This poetic autobiography is grounded in the poet's relationship with his mother.

Lewis, J. Patrick and Yolen, Jane. 2012. *Take Two! A Celebration of Twins.*
*Playful, whimsical poems salute the special relationship between twins.

Mora, Pat. Ed. 2001. *Love to Mamá: A Tribute to Mothers.*
*Thirteen poets celebrate the bonds we have with mothers and grandmothers.

Salas, Laura Purdie. 2018. *Meet My Family! Animal Babies and Their Families.*
*Both rhyming and informative, learn about all kinds of animal families.

Singer, Marilyn. 1994. *Family Reunion.*
*A fun celebration of the colorful characters that gather for a family reunion.

Smith, Hope Anita. 2009. *Mother Poems.*
*Poems share grief at the loss of a mother, as well as honor her strength and love.

Walker, Rob D. 2009. *Mama Says: A Book of Love for Mothers and Sons*
*A poetic tribute to the wisdom of mothers.

Weatherford, Carole Boston. 2021. *Dreams for a Daughter.*
*A poetic love letter from mother to daughter.

Wong, Janet S. 2021. *Good Luck Gold & MORE.*
*The first book of poetry for young people to explore Asian American identity.

Wong, Janet S. 2019. *A Suitcase of Seaweed & MORE.*
*Poems and prose look at Korean, Chinese, and American elements in the life of an Asian American family.

POETS WRITE ABOUT WRITING

Several poets have written books ABOUT poetry writing for young people. Here are a few that might be helpful.

Fletcher, Ralph J. 2005. *A Writing Kind of Day: Poems for Young Poets.*
*How to write a poem about almost anything, with tips on every step of the creative process.

Holbrook, Sara, Salinger, Michael and Harvey, Stephanie. 2018. *From Striving to Thriving Writers: Strategies that Jump-Start Writing.*
*Twenty-seven writing strategies and lessons targeting reading, writing, and speaking.

Janeczko, Paul B., comp. 2002. *Seeing the Blue Between: Advice and Inspiration for Young Poets.*
*A poetry collection with poems and advice from 32 poets.

Lawson, JonArno. 2008. *Inside Out: Children's Poets Discuss Their Work.*
*Twenty-three poets sharing poems and explaining how the poem came to be.

Prelutsky, Jack. 2008. *Pizza, Pigs, and Poetry: How to Write a Poem.*
*The poet sharing how he creates poems from anecdotes, often using comic exaggeration.

Salas, Laura Purdie. 2011. *Picture Yourself Writing Poetry: Using Photos to Inspire Writing.*
*A clear and engaging approach with writing prompts and mentor texts.

Wolf, Allan. 2006. *Immersed in Verse: An Informative, Slightly Irreverent & Totally Tremendous Guide to Living the Poet's Life.*
*A poet toolbox full of fun facts, playful writing activities, and words of wisdom and encouragement.

Wong, Janet. 2002. *You Have to Write.*
*A poem picture book emphasizing revision and writing about everyday experiences.

Meet the Author series (published by Richard C. Owen)
Picture books in the "Meet the Author" series feature poets like Douglas Florian, Lee Bennett Hopkins, Janet Wong, and Jane Yolen talking about their lives and how they write poetry.

PLACES TO PUBLISH POETRY

Here are a variety of print and online sources that include poetry by young writers. Be sure to check the rules and specifications for submitting in each venue. Give it a try, have fun, and good luck!

Creative Kids (ages 8-16)
http://www.ckmagazine.org
*"The nation's largest magazine for and by kids."

Carus Publishing (Cicada, Cobblestone, Faces, Dig, Muse) (ages 9-14+)
http://www.cobblestonepub.com/index.html
*Magazines on topics from nature to history and more.

New Moon: The Magazine for Girls and Their Dreams (ages 8-14)
http://www.newmoon.com/
*Special online community and magazine for girls.

Skipping Stones (all ages)
http://www.skippingstones.org
*International, multicultural, environmental magazine.

The Claremont Review (ages 13-19)
http://www.theclaremontreview.ca
*International magazine based in Canada.

Stone Soup (ages 8-13)
http://stonesoup.com
*Stories, poems, book reviews, and artwork by young people.

The Telling Room (ages 6-18)
http://www.tellingroom.org/stories
*Publications of annual anthologies, chapbooks, and on the web.

Canvas (ages 8-13)
http://canvasliteraryjournal.com
*Published in print, ebook, web, video, and audio formats.

Writing (grades 7-12)
http://classroommagazines.scholastic.com
*Monthly publication, writing prompts and writing contests.

PUBLISHED POETRY BY YOUNG WRITERS

Here are several notable collections of poetry written by young people.

Lowe, Ayana. Ed. 2008. *Come and Play: Children of Our World Having Fun.*
*Here are photos of children around the world along with poems by young writers, ages 5-11.

Lyne, Sandford. Ed. 2004. *Soft Hay Will Catch You.*
*Kentucky poet Lyne gathers poems by young writers about home and family.

McLaughlin, Timothy. Ed. 2012. *Walking on Earth and Touching the Sky: Poetry and Prose by Lakota Youth at Red Cloud Indian School.*
*Powerful prose blends with personal poetry by Lakota students at Red Cloud Indian School in South Dakota.

Nye, Naomi Shihab. Ed. 2000. *Salting the Ocean: 100 Poems by Young Poets.*
*Nye collected "100 poems by 100 poets in grades one through twelve."

Simon, John O. Ed. 2011. *Cyclops Wearing Flip-Flops.*
*Students in grades 3-8 respond to classic poems and write their own.

Spain, Sahara Sunday. 2001. *If There Would Be No Light: Poems from My Heart.*
*Dig into these poems by a nine-year-old who has traveled the world.

Stepanek, Mattie. 2002. *Heartsongs.*
*This young poet writes about living with illness and loss.

POETRY WRITING CHECKLIST

Poets of all ages often need guidance in looking at their own work critically. A checklist or guidelines can be helpful in developing skill in revising one's own writing. No single list is perfect, nor is each step necessary every time, but checklists can be a good revision tool. Here is one example created by poetry teacher Aaren Perry that includes questions you might find helpful.

Perry's Self-Questioning Guidelines

1. What can I put in my poem?
    *Who, what, when, where, why, how?
    *Sight, sound, smell, feel, taste?

2. Are there things I would like to fix?
    *Line breaks?
    *Punctuation, spelling?
    *The title?
    *The beginning, middle, end?

3. Maybe I could add more...

4. Maybe I don't need that word.

5. How does this look on the page?

6. How will this sound when I read it out loud?
    *Rhythm, rhyme, movement?
    *Loud? Quiet? Both?

Based on: Perry, Aaren Yeatts. 1997. *Poetry Across the Curriculum: An Action Guide for Elementary Teachers.* Boston: Allyn & Bacon, p. 183.

KINDS OF POEMS

There are several different types of poems in this book, including the following. Just for fun, try writing your own poem in one of these forms.

Acrostic Poem ("Tutor" p. 73)
An acrostic poem uses the first letter of the first word of each line to create a word vertically that is often the theme or topic of the poem.

Free Verse Poem ("Wedding" p. 13; "Classroom" p. 21; "Puppies!"; p. 27)
Poets who write free verse poems do not use rhyme at the ends of lines, but they often create a rhythm with the length of lines.

List Poem ("Smoocheroos" p. 57; "Hope" p. 67)
A list poem incorporates a list of items important to the poem topic.

Mask Poem ("Suitcase" p. 81)
A mask poem is written from the point of view of an object, an animal, or a person that is not you (the writer).

Metaphor Poem ("Forecast" p. 79)
The poem compares one thing to another thing that is usually unrelated, but shares attributes.

Poem with Repetition ("Together" p. 25' "Troop" p. 53)
Poets often repeat a word or phrase or line to emphasize the meaning or to maximize the sounds of the words.

Poem with Rhythm ("Wish" p. 59, "Rivals" p. 98)
The poem has a very strong beat of stressed (and unstressed) syllables.

Poem with Simile ("Roots" p. 49; "Hive" p. 33)
A poem where two or more things are compared with the words "like" or "as" (often a person compared with an animal or object).

Rhyming Poem ("Family" p. 9; "Cousins" p. 15; "Grandma" p. 43)
Many poets use rhyme to emphasize the sounds of words – at the end of lines, in alternating lines, or even in the middle of lines.

Shape Poem ("Balance" p. 47)
The words of the poem are arranged in a shape to suggest the poem's subject.

POETRY AWARDS AND BEST LISTS

There are several major awards given to poets and works of poetry. Knowing about these awards can help you choose what is considered high-quality work.

The **Young People's Poet Laureate (YPPL)** recognizes a poet for her/his body of work. The YPPL consults with the Poetry Foundation and raises awareness of the power of poetry for young people.

Another major award for poetry for children is the **National Council of Teachers of English (NCTE) Award for Excellence in Poetry for Children**, given to a poet for her or his entire body of work in writing or anthologizing poetry for children. Janet Wong is a recent winner of this prestigious award.

Other prominent awards include **The Lee Bennett Hopkins Award for Children's Poetry**, which is presented annually by Pennsylvania State University to an American poet or anthologist for the most outstanding new book of children's poetry published in the previous year.

The Lee Bennett Hopkins/ILA Promising Poet Award goes to a poet with one or two published books, and aims to encourage new poets.

The Claudia Lewis Award is given annually by Bank Street College to the best poetry book of the year.

The Lion and the Unicorn Award for Excellence in North American Poetry is given annually to the best poetry book published in either the U.S. or Canada.

The CYBILS Award (Children's & Young Adult Bloggers' Literary Awards) is given annually to a book of poetry for young people as well as to a novel in verse.

The NCTE Excellence in Poetry Award Committee selects an annual list of **NCTE Poetry Notables** including both poetry books and verse novels.

The CL/R SIG of the International Literacy Association selects an annual list of **Notable Books for a Global Society** for enhancing understanding of world cultures and often includes poetry.

ABOUT THE POETS

You probably found some favorite poems when reading this book. Write down the poets' names and learn more about them by visiting their websites and blogs. Then look for more of their poems (and books)!

Alma Flor Ada   almaflorada.com
Dr. Alma Flor Ada, awarded numerous national and international honors, is a leader and mentor in bilingual education whose writing ranges from poetry for the very young to adult novels. She loves her unique family.

Gail Aldous   scbwi.org/members-public/gail-aldous
Former teacher Gail Aldous is a writer for children and teens whose poems appear in *What Is a Friend?* and *Things We Eat*. Gail loves hiking with her family.

Alexia M. Andoni   alexiamandoni.com
Alexia M. Andoni is a teacher, poet, and children's book author. She grew up in a large family resembling a grove, where she felt supported by its roots and held high by its branches.

Chris Baron   chris-baron.com
Chris Baron is the award-winning author of *The Magical Imperfect*, *All of Me*, and *The Gray*. He is a Professor of English at San Diego City College and the director of the Writing Center. He lives in San Diego with his wife and kids where he's trying his best to tend to his family roots.

Willeena Booker   Twitter: @WilleenaB
Willeena Booker is an inspiring educator, poet, and advocate of social justice. Her poems appear in *What Is a Friend?* and *Things We Feel*. Willeena loves a reunion anytime friends, family, and poets gather together!

Sandy Brehl   sandybrehlbooks.com
Sandy Brehl's books include the *Odin's Promise* trilogy (WWII resistance story in Norway), a picture book, *Is It Over?*, and poetry. Like her characters, Sandy takes shelter in family and stories.

Judy Bryan   judybryanauthor.com
Judy Bryan is a children's author and poet. She has fond memories of being a Girl Scout, including camping, hiking, and roasting marshmallows over a campfire for yummy s'mores!

Elenore Byrne   elenorewrites.wordpress.com
Elenore Byrne writes children's poetry and picture books. Her publication credits include *PaperBound Magazine*, *The Dirigible Balloon*, *Clubhouse Jr. Magazine*, and the *Chasing Clouds* and *10.10* poetry anthologies. She lives in Switzerland with a young family who all enjoy storytime.

F. Isabel Campoy   isabelcampoy.com
F. Isabel Campoy, author of more than 80 books including *Maybe Something Beautiful* and *Yes! We Are Latinos*, writes poems in three languages and enjoys inventing words such as "famylous."

Kate Coombs   katecoombs.com
Kate Coombs grew up near the ocean. She doesn't have an orca poem in her award-winning book of ocean poems, *Water Sings Blue*, so she was happy to write one!

Cynthia Cotten   cynthiacotten.com
Cynthia Cotten is a poet and author of nine books, including *Snow Ponies* and *This Is the Stable*. Some days she feels old like Granny, but with a better paint job.

Mary E. Cronin   maryecronin.com
Mary E. Cronin is a K-2 Literacy Coach whose poetry has appeared in several anthologies and in *The New York Times*. Her best childhood memories are of birthday parties, cakes, and cousins.

Leslie Degnan   Twitter: @degnanleslie
Leslie Degnan is a former early childhood educator who writes poetry and picture books for children. She loves to laugh with family and friends and enjoys learning new things, especially secret handshakes!

Janet Clare Fagal   Facebook: facebook.com/janet.clare.311
Retired teacher Janet Clare Fagal is a poet and poetry advocate. Born to a musician father, she once played glockenspiel in her high school band in the Cherry Blossom Parade in Washington, D.C.

Theresa Gaughan   Twitter: @TheresaGaughan
Theresa Gaughan is a veteran teacher who enjoys writing and sharing poetry with her third-grade students. Whenever she travels, she makes sure her suitcase contains cozy pajamas and her favorite books.

Rajani LaRocca   rajanilarocca.com
Rajani LaRocca, author of numerous picture books and middle grade novels, including *Red, White, and Whole*, a Walter Award and Newbery Honor winner, finds endless inspiration in her family.

Renée M. LaTulippe   reneelatulippe.com
Renée M. LaTulippe writes poetry, picture books, and verse novels and is the founder of the Lyrical Language Lab. She always cries at weddings, even if she doesn't know the people.

Rebecca Gardyn Levington   rebeccagardynlevington.com
Rebecca Gardyn Levington is the author of the picture books *Brainstorm!* and *Whatever Comes Tomorrow*, as well as many poems. She is grateful for her family, whose encouraging words help her remember: *Yes, she can!*

Molly Lorenz   Twitter: @booksR4me
Molly Lorenz is a member of SCBWI and a retired art teacher. She has been published in *Things We Do*, *What Is a Friend?*, and *Things We Wear*. She grew up in a family with four sisters and everybody had their chores.

Rochelle Melander   rochellemelander.com
Writing coach and artist educator Rochelle Melander is the author of 12 books, including *Mightier Than the Sword*. She plays tune-up with her writing and catch-up with her reading list.

Jack Prelutsky   poetryfoundation.org/poets/jack-prelutsky
Jack Prelutsky, Children's Poet Laureate from 2006-2008, is the author of several dozen poetry collections and anthologies, including *Hard-Boiled Bugs for Breakfast*. His memories of his grandmother include the mass quantities of bacon she fed him.

Joan Riordan   Twitter: @JRiordan173
Joan Riordan is an early childhood educator with decades of experience who once took a large teddy bear food shopping. She enjoys practicing yoga for flexibility and balance.

Donna JT Smith   mainelywrite.blogspot.com
Donna JT Smith, a long-time teacher, has poems in many anthologies, including *What Is a Friend?* and *Things We Eat*. She writes from the comfort of her hive by the sea!

Anastasia Suen   asuen.com
Anastasia Suen is the author (and ghostwriter) of more than 400 books for children, teens, and adults. Her kindergarten to college teaching career began with tutoring at home.

Pamela Taylor   pamelabtaylor.com
A former educator, Pamela Taylor now writes picture books and has featured poems included in *Things We Feel* and *What Is a Friend?* Her passion for poetry has no rivals!

Joyce Uglow   inkingcompellingstories.com
Joyce Uglow writes poetic stories on topics from bees, trees, and families to ancient cave art and fossils trapped in asphalt seeps. She's a forever cheerleader for Team Education.

Fernanda Valentino   Twitter: @fgvalentino
Fernanda Valentino was raised in Perth, Australia and now lives in South Loop, Chicago. She translates books and poetry from French to English, and her poems have appeared in *Highlights Hello!* and *High Five Magazine*. Butterfly kisses were her son's favorite kisses when he was a child.

April Halprin Wayland   aprilwayland.com
April Halprin Wayland is an author, poet, and teacher in the UCLA Extension Writers' Program, where she won Instructor of the Year. Her goal is for each class to become a family.

Vicki Wilke   winningwriters.com/people/vicki-wilke
Vicki Wilke taught K-1 for 33 years, and continues to write poetry for children and adults. She loves time with her five precious grandchildren, and is expecting many more years of poetry joy!

Matthew Winter   Twitter: @Baileysdad420
Matthew Winter is a first-grade teacher in New York who loves writing poems and reading. He finds love, peace, comfort, joy, harmony, and hope in his poodle-son Bailey.

Helen Kemp Zax   helenzax.com
Helen Kemp Zax is a former lawyer whose poems have been published in anthologies such as *What Is a Family?* and *Imperfect II*. Her favorite part of every birthday is making a wish she hopes will come true.

POEM CREDITS

Alma Flor Ada: "We"; © 2023 by Alma Flor Ada.
Gail Aldous: "Glad"; © 2023 by Gail Aldous.
Alexia M. Andoni: "Grove"; © 2023 by Alexia M. Andoni.
Chris Baron: "Roots"; © 2023 by Chris Baron.
Willeena Booker: "Reunion"; © 2023 by Willeena Booker.
Sandy Brehl: "Forecast"; © 2023 by Sandy Brehl.
Judy Bryan: "Troop"; © 2023 by Judy Bryan.
Elenore Byrne: "Storytime"; © 2023 by Elenore Byrne.
F. Isabel Campoy: "Joy"; © 2023 by F. Isabel Campoy.
Kate Coombs: "Orcas"; © 2023 by Kate Coombs.
Mary E. Cronin: "Cousins"; © 2023 by Mary E. Cronin.
Leslie Degnan: "Handshake" and "Laughter"; © 2023 by Leslie Degnan.
Janet Clare Fagal: "Band"; © 2023 by Janet Clare Fagal.
Theresa Gaughan: "Suitcase"; © 2023 by Theresa Gaughan.
Rajani LaRocca: "Family"; © 2023 by Rajani LaRocca.
Renée M. LaTulippe: "Wedding"; © 2022 by Renée M. LaTulippe.
Rebecca Gardyn Levington: "Encouragement"; © 2023 by Rebecca Gardyn Levington.
Molly Lorenz: "Chores"; © 2023 by Marilyn Lorenz.
Rochelle Melander: "Catch-up" and "Tune-up"; © 2023 by Rochelle Melander.
Jack Prelutsky: "Grandma"; © 2023 by Jack Prelutsky.
Joan Riordan: "Balance" and "Stuffies"; © 2023 by Joan Riordan.
Donna JT Smith: "Carousel" and "Hive"; © 2023 by Donna JT Smith.
Anastasia Suen: "TUTOR"; © 2023 by Anastasia Suen.
Pamela Taylor: "Rivals"; © 2023 by Pamela Taylor.
Joyce Uglow: "Together"; © 2023 by Joyce Uglow.
Fernanda Valentino: "Smoocheroos"; © 2023 by Fernanda Valentino.
April Halprin Wayland: "Classroom" and "Puppies!"; © 2023 by April Halprin Wayland.
Vicki Wilke: "Expecting"; © 2023 by Vicki Wilke.
Matthew Winter: "Hope"; © 2023 by Matthew Winter.
Janet Wong: "Goodbye," "IBBY," "Searching," and "Sharing"; © 2023 by Janet S. Wong.
Helen Kemp Zax: "Wish"; © 2023 by Helen Kemp Zax.

ABOUT VARDELL & WONG

Sylvia M. Vardell recently retired as Professor in the School of Library and Information Studies at Texas Woman's University where she taught graduate courses in children's and young adult literature for more than 20 years. Vardell has published extensively, including five books on literature for children as well as over 25 book chapters and 100 journal articles. In her spare time, she loves going to Star Wars conventions with her family - all in costumes. Learn more about Vardell at SylviaVardell.com.

Janet Wong is a graduate of Yale Law School and a former lawyer. She has written more than 40 books for children on a wide variety of subjects, including chess (*Alex and the Wednesday Chess Club*) and yoga (*Twist: Yoga Poems*). She is the 2021 winner of the NCTE Excellence in Poetry for Children Award, a lifetime achievement award that is one of the highest honors a children's poet can receive. Janet and her husband moved recently from New Jersey to Washington state to be closer to family. Learn more about Janet at Janet-Wong.com.

Together, Vardell & Wong are the creative forces behind Pomelo Books, a publisher whose "family" of authors includes more than 250 poets.

ABOUT POMELO BOOKS

Pomelo Books is Poetry PLUS. Poetry PLUS play. Poetry PLUS science. Poetry PLUS holidays. Poetry PLUS pets – and more. We make It EASY to share poetry any time of day.

Successful K-12 teachers and administrators build regular "touch points" into their routines to create a safe and engaging learning environment. Poetry can be a powerful tool for offering a shared literary experience in just a few minutes, with both curricular benefits and emotional connections for students at all levels.

Our books in *The Poetry Friday Anthology* series and the *Poetry Friday Power Book* series make it easy to use poetry for integrating skills, building language learning, crossing curricular areas, mentoring young writers, promoting critical thinking, fostering social-emotional development, and inviting students to respond creatively. A shared poetry moment can help build a classroom community filled with kindness, respect, and joy. Learn more at PomeloBooks.com.

The Poetry of Science
An NSTA Recommends selection
"A treasury of the greatest science poetry for children ever written, with a twist." NSTA

The Poetry of Science is an illustrated book for children that contains 250 poems on science, technology, engineering, and math organized by topic.

Great Morning! Poems for School Leaders to Read Aloud
A CBC Hot Off the Press selection

75 poems for morning announcements or for the start of class or just to take a "brain break" when you need it! Principals, teachers, and student leaders will find poems on many useful topics from school safety to celebrating the teamwork of teachers and staff members such as the school nurse or custodian.

HERE WE GO: A Poetry Friday Power Book
An NCTE Poetry Notable
An NNSTOY Social Justice Book

How can kids change the world? By practicing kindness, raising a garden that unites a community, thinking about the news, and more. This story in poems (with activities to get us drawing, talking, and writing) will guide kids as they discover their power to make an impact.

MORE FROM POMELO BOOKS

HOP TO IT: Poems to Get You Moving
A Kids' Book Choice Award "Best Book of Facts" Winner

This anthology of 100 poems by 90 poets gets kids thinking and moving as they use pantomime, sign language, and whole body movements, including deskercise! You'll also find poems on "21st-century" topics, such as life during a pandemic. Take a 30-second indoor recess whenever you need it!

The Poetry Friday Anthology for Celebrations
ILA Notable Books for a Global Society

This fun book features 156 poems (in both Spanish & English) honoring a wide variety of traditional and non-traditional holidays from all over the world. Also available in a Teacher/Librarian Edition.

"A bubbly and educational bilingual poetry anthology for children." – Kirkus

What Is a Friend?
A CBC Hot Off the Press selection

Forty-one poems by recognized poets and new talents explore the many aspects of friendship, including friendship with pets, teammates as friends, friends who are family members, and much more.

YOU JUST WAIT: A Poetry Friday Power Book
A CBC Hot Off the Press selection
An NCTE Poetry Notable

Twelve poems by poets such as Joseph Bruchac and Margarita Engle are joined into a story with poems about identity, sports, food, and movies.

"Young readers will find their fingers itching to respond to these verses." – Carol Jago, Past President of NCTE

Made in the USA
Monee, IL
08 April 2023

31565102R00059